ISBN 978-0-484-33030-5
PIBN 10305963

GOAL SETTING AND

SELF-DIRECTED BEHAVIOR CHANGE[1]

David A. Kolb and Richard E. Boyatzis

349-68

[1]Not to be quoted or reporduced in any form prior to publication. We wish to express our appreciation to William McKelvey, Sara Winter, James Curtis and Robert Zuckerman for assistance in research design and administeration, and to Robert Euritt, George Farris, Michael Fulenwider, William McKelvey, Irwin Rubin, Suresh Srivastra and Sara Winter who served as T-Group trainers, and to the students who through their efforts made this research possible.

Two recent developments, one theoretical and one practical, have led behavior change researchers to pay more attention to self-directed techniques of behavior change. In practice, there is a growing demand for behavioral science solutions to human problems. More and more individuals are seeing that the various forms of psychotherapy can provide viable solutions to their personal problems. In addition, social welfare agencies are seeking to change their role from that of policeman and distributor of government funds to that of an agent for individual and community development. This growing demand for the practical application of behavioral science knowledge has made practicioners painfully aware of the fact that, using the existing techniques of behavior change which are so dependent on the change agent for their success, there can never be enough professionally trained personnel to meet this demand. So in desperation the practicioner is asking, "How crucial am I in the change process? Is is possible to develop change techniques that people can use themselves?"

Until recently the theoretical answer has been no. Therapeutic models of change, both the analytic and learning theory based, have conceived of the patient as passive and reactive. In the tradition of their medical origins it is the doctor who was the active and curative agent in the therapeutic process. By its choice of Watson and the behaviorist tradition over the psychologies of William James and E.B. Titchner, American psychology came to emphasize the control and measurement of behavior and to ignore the role of man's consciousness. Behaviorists and Freudian psychologists ignored the proactive aspect of man's nature in favor of reactive theories which reduce human consciousness to an epiphenomenon controlled by powerful forces of behavioral conditioning or unconscious instincts. The concept of will -- man's ability to consciously control and change his own behavior -- was nowhere to

be found in respectable psychological theories. The idea of self-directed change appeared only in common sense psychologics like those of Norman Vincent Peale and Dale Carnegie.

Evidence for how much the reactive side of man has been emphasized over the proactive can be seen in the results of a small study by Gorden Allport (1960).

> What we did, in brief, was to study the frequency of the prefixes re- and pro- in psychological language. Our hypothesis was that re- compounds, connoting as they do again-ness, passivity, being pushed or maneuvered, would be far more common than pro- compounds connoting futurity, intention, forward thrust. Our sample consisted of the indices of the Psychological abstracts at five-year intervals over the past thirty years; also, all terms employing these prefixes in Hinsie and Shatzky's Psychiatric dictionary and in English and English's Psychological dictionary. In addition, we made a random sampling of pages in five current pyschological journals. Combining these sources, it turns out that re- compounds are nearly five times as numerous as pro- compounds.
>
> But, of course, not every compound is relevant to our purpose. Terms like reference, relationship, reticular, report do not have the connotation we seek; nor do terms like probability, process and propaganda. Our point is more clearly seen when we note that the term reaction or reactive occurs hundreds of times, while the term proaction or proactive occurs only once -- and that in English's Dictionary, in spite of the fact that Harry Murray has made an effort to introduce the word into psychological usage.
>
> But even if we attempt a more strict coding of this lexical material, accepting only those terms that clearly imply reaction and response on one side and proaction or the progressive programming of behavior on the other, we find the ratio still is approximately 5:1. In other words, our vocabulary is five times richer in terms like reaction, response, reinforcement, reflex, respondent, retroactive, recognition, regression, repression, reminiscence than in terms like production, proceeding , proficiency, problem-solving, propriate and programming. So much for the number of different words available. The disproportion is more striking when we note that the four terms reflex, reaction, response, and retention together are used one hundred times more frequently than any single pro- compound except problem-solving and projective -- and this latter term I submit, is ordinarily used only in the sense of reactivity (p. 40-41).

Currently, however, there are a great number of theorists who challenge the reactive conception of man. Hartmann, Kris and Loewenstein (1947) and

other ego psychologists began to reinterpret psychoanalytic theory placing increasing emphasis on the power of ego processes in the rational direction and control of one's behavior. More recently White (1959) has detailed the research evidence for pro-active, competence motivation in human beings -- motives urging men and animals to ignore safety and security, and to take on new, difficult, and challenging tasks. Of these theorists it is perhaps Carl Rogers who has been most influential in applying the new growth-oriented theory of man to the practice of behavior change. He created a new theory and method of psychotherapy -- client-centered therapy (1951). As the name implies, in client-centered therapy the client is the active and curative agent in the therapeutic relationship. The therapist's job is to create in a non-directive way the therapeutic conditions which will facilitate self-inquiry and personal growth in the client. By emphasizing man's creative and problem solving abilities and his growth potential the pro-active theorists imply that self-directed change is not only theoretically possible but that it occurs as a natural life process.

These two conflicting models of man pose something of a dilemma, for we cannot accept one and discard the other without doing an injustice to the data. Research evidence and common sense observations can be marshalled to support both theories -- man is passive and controlled by his environment as well as creative and self-directing. the noted ethologist Konrad Lorenz (1963) suggests, however, that this dilemma is an illusion. There is no contradiction, he maintains, between the fact that man's behavior is governed by causal stimulus-response type laws and the fact that man strives toward goals and can modify his behavior by an act of will. "The appreciation of the fact that life processes are directed at aims or goals, and the realization of the other fact that they are, at the same time, determined by causality, not only do

not preclude each other but they only make sense in combination. If man did not strive toward goals, his questions as to causes would have no sense; if he has no insight into cause and effect, he is powerless to guide effects toward determined goals, however rightly he may have understood the meaning of these goals... (p. 231). Increasing knowledge of the natural causes of his own behavior can certainly increase a man's faculties and enable him to put his free will into action... (p. 232)." Thus, in his integration of the two models of man Lorenz suggests a methodology for self-directed change. If we can increase an individual's understanding of the psychological laws which govern his behavior, we can increase his capacity for self-direction. In the spirit of Lorenz's insight, the research program of which this study is a part is attempting to create a simple method for self-directed behavior change that will serve as a paradigm for studying those factors which are crucial in the process of self-direction.

The method employed in a self-directed change project is very simple. The major emphasis is on self-research. Each subject is encouraged to reflect on his own behavior, and to select a limited and well-defined goal which he would like to achieve. The next step is to undertake a continuing and accurate assessment of his behavior in the area related to his change goal. He keeps an objective record of his behavior in this area, generally in the form of a graph which measures progress toward the goal from day to day. The subject decides for himself how long the project should continue and when his goal is attained.

When business-school students used this method to change themselves as part of their participation in self-analytic groups (Kolb, Winter and Berlew, 1968), two factors were found that predicted the students' success in changing. Change was found to be related to the individual's commitment to his

change goal and the amount of feedback he received from other group members during the last half of the group. Improving the change method to increase goal commitment and feedback increased the percentage of students successfully attaining their goals from 5% to 61%.

The research reported in this paper is a more detailed exploration of the dynamics of the goal-setting process in self-directed behavior change. More specifically, we seek answers to the following questions:

1. Does conscious goal-setting facilitate goal achievement?
2. What characteristics of the goal-setting process are related to subsequent success or failure in goal-achievement?

Goal-Setting and Goal-Achievement

There has been a great deal of attention given to the relationship between goal-setting and goal-achievement in the psychological literature. Most of these studies, however, have been conducted in the level of aspiration experimental paradigm and have been concerned mainly with the question -- How does successful or unsuccessful goal-achievement affect goal-setting? (Lewin _et.al_. 1944, Festinger 1942, Frank 1941). The major result of these studies has been that success increases aspirations and failure to a lesser extent decreases aspirations. Comparatively little attention has been given to the reverse question which is central to understanding the role of goal setting in self-directed behavior change -- How does goal-setting affect success in goal-achievement?

To understand the role of conscious goal-setting in behavior change we must return to William James, whose essay on will stands today as psychology's major contribution to our understanding of how consciousness controls behavior. James' theory of the will is based on his ideo-motor theory of action -- that

any idea fixed in consciousness will automatically issue forth into action. It follows from this theory that ideas that hold conscious attention will control behavior. "It seems as if we ought to look for the secret of an idea's impulsiveness, not in any particular relations which it may have with paths of motor discharge for all ideas have relations with some such paths -- but rather in a preliminary phenomenon, the urgency, namely with which it is able to compel attention and dominate in consciousness... (p. 391)". The essential achievement of the will, in short, when it is most voluntary, is to attend to a difficult object and hold it fast before the mind... Effort of attention is thus the essential phenomenon of the will... (p. 393, 1963)". In his description of the strong-willed man James describes this process:

> The strong-willed man, however, is the man who hears the still small voice unflinchingly, and who, when the death-bringing consideration comes, looks at its face, consents to its presence, clings to it, affirms it, and holds it fast, in spite of the host of exciting mental images which rise in revolt against it and would expel it from the mind. Sustained in this way by a resolute effort of attention, the difficult object erelong begins to call up its own cogeners and associates and ends by changing the disposition of the man's consciousness altogether. And with his consciousness his action changes, for the new object, once stably in possession of the field of his thoughts, infallibly produces its own motor effects. The difficulty lies in the gaining possession of that field. Though the spontaneous drift of thought is all the other way, the attention must be kept strained on that one object until at last it grows, so as to maintain itself before the mind with ease. This strain of the attention is the fundamental act of will. And the will's work is in most cases practically ended when the bare presence to our thought of the natrually unwelcome object has been secured. For the mysterious tie between the thought and the motor centers next comes into play, and in a way which we cannot even guess at, the obediency of the bodily organs follows as a matter of course.
>
> In all this one sees how the immediate point of application of the volitional effort lies exclusively in the mental world. The whole drama is a mental drama. The whole difficulty is a mental difficulty, difficulty with an ideal object of our thought. It is, in one word, an idea to which our will applies itself, an idea which if we let it go would slip away, but which we will not let go. Consent to the idea's undivided presence, this is effort's sole achievement (1963, p. 394).

Thus we see that willing to achieve a goal is basically an art of attending to that goal until it becomes dominant in consciousness; and when this occurs, change toward the goal will follow. What experimental evidence can be mustered to support this theory?

A modern counterpart to James' theory can be found in McClelland's theory of motivation. Motives in his theory are affectively toned associative networks arranged in a hierarchy of impacture within the individual (McClelland, 1965). In other words a motive is an emotionally toned pattern of thinking. The influence which a motive holds over an individual's behavior is determined by the extent to which this pattern of thinking dominates an individual's consciousness. Hundreds of studies have been conducted within this theoretical framework showing the relationship between achievement motivation and behavior as well as other motives such as power, affiliation, aggression and sex (McClelland, 1961; Atkinson, 1957). In addition a number of behavior change programs have reported success in changing achievement motivated behavior by changing (among other things) the position of the achievement motive in a person's motive heirarchy by helping him develop and clearly conceptualize the associative network defining the motive (Kolb 1965, McClelland 1965, Litwin and Aronoff, in press). These studies all lend support to the notion that dominance of a goal (i.e., achievement desires) in consciousness will lead to behavior toward that goal (i.e., achievement related behavior).

Managerial psychology provides another source of evidence for the importance of conscious goal setting for goal achievement. The field has long recognized the importance of goal setting and recent programs of management by objectives have made this process quite explicit in industrial management (Drucker 1954). Studies of organizations have shown productivity and efficiency is almost always greater when the worker sets his own goals

(Likert 1967, McGregor 1960). One excellent field study of performance appraisal interviews by Kay, French and Myer (1962) gives empirical support to the hypothesis that conscious goal setting leads to goal achievement. The authors found that when managers' improvement needs were translated into specific goals during performance appraisal interviews, 65.2% of these goals were subsequently achieved. When improvement needs were not translated into specific goals only 27.3% were subsequently accomplished. Kay and French conclude that, "Appreciable improvements in performance were realized only when specific goals were established with time deadlines set and results measures agreed upon. Regardless of how much emphasis the manager gave to an improvement need in the appraisal discussion, if this did not get translated into a specific goal, very little performance improvement was achieved" (p. 1).

Two studies in the level of aspiration literature have attempted to show the effect that stating a level of aspiration has a subsequent performance. Kausler (1959) gave a simple arithmetic test to three groups of students, two of which were asked to state levels of aspiration. He found that when mathematical ability was held constant those who were asked to state their level of aspiration performed significantly better than those who were not. Rao (1956) conducted an experiment in which he examined the effects of level of aspiration and feedback on performance. His conclusion was that task performance was decreased when either a level of aspiration was not stated or feedback was withheld.

Finally, our previous research on self-directed behavior change (Kolb, Winter and Berlew 1968) suggested that when the self-directed change method was modified to emphasize conscious goal setting the percent of successful goal achievement increased from 44% to 61%.

There is, then, some empirical support for the hypothesis that conscious goal-setting facilitates goal-achievement. The purpose of the study reported here is to assertain whether conscious goal-setting will facilitate the achievement of personal improvement goals by individuals using the self-directed behavior change method. To state the hypothesis more formally:

> Hypothesis I. Individuals will change more on those dimensions of their self-concept which they define as relevant to their consciously set change goal than they will on dimensions of their self-concept which they define as not relevant. This difference will be independent of the difficulty of the change goal.

This hypothesis differs from those of previously reported research in that it does not involve an experimental manipulation of the independent variable, goal-setting. This difference overcomes one problem with previous research designs but creates another. The problem with the previous experimental designs is that it is impossible to determine whether the improvements in performance were a result of conscious goal-setting or a result of the influence attempts of the experimenter which are inherent in asking an individual to set goals. By asking a person to say how many arithmetic problems he is going to do or by defining with him what specifically he is going to do to improve his job performance the experimenter or manager is in effect telling the person to achieve the goal. Research on the social psychology of experimental situations suggests that this influence, even if unconscious, can be very great (Milgram 1968, Orne 1962, Rosenthal 1963). In the current experiment, subjects are free to choose whatever goal they wish thus eliminating effect of experimenter persuasion. The problem with the current design, however, is that it is difficult to conclude that it is conscious goal-setting that causes greater goal achievement. Individuals may simply choose goals that are easier to achieve. In an attempt to overcome this problem we will test whether goal-setting facilitates change in difficult as well as easy goals.

Characteristics of the Goal-Setting Process

In addition to assessing the effect of conscious goal-setting on goal achievement this research seeks to determine those characteristics of the goal-setting process which facilitate goal achievement. From a content analysis of individuals' initial goal statements five hypotheses will be tested. These include an exploration of the individual's awareness of his goal, his expectation of success, and his level of pyschological safety. The remaining two hypotheses are concerned with the individual's evaluation of his progress -- the extent to which he proposes to measure his progress and the degree to which he controls his own reinforcement and evaluates himself.

Awareness. Implicit in William James' theory of the will is the hypothesis that awareness of a goal will be positively related to achievement of the goal. The more a goal dominates an individual's consciousness the more he will be likely to strive toward that goal. Similarly, most forms of psychotherapy attempt to increase the patient's awareness of the forces affecting his behavior with the implicit assumption that this insight will change the patient's behavior. Two recent psychotherapy research programs have been able to define the role of awareness in personality change more specifically. Gendlin, *et.al.* (1968) has devised a process measure of what he calls the client's ability. He describes the rate of focusing ability in therapy as follows,

> The therapist calls the client's attention to an as yet unclear partly cognitive and situational complex which is concretely felt by the client. The client must then be willing and able to focus his attention directly on this felt complex so that he can concretely feel and struggle with it (p. 218).

Gendlin finds that clients who display this kind of focusing ability in therapy interviews improve after therapy while those who do not show focusing

ability do not improve. Truax and Carkhuff (1964) have developed a process measure which they call interpersonal exploration that is similar to focusing ability in that it emphasizes awareness of feelings associated with ones problems. They also find that presence of interpersonal exploration in psychotherapy interviews is indicative of successful change.

In a study of the personality characteristics of individuals who are successful in self-directed behavior change projects Winter, Griffith and Kolb (1968) found results that suggest that successful change is a function of one's ability to maintain awareness of the dissonance between one's ideal self and ones current self.

Thus we are led to hypothesize:

> Hypothesis II. Individuals who are successful in achieving their change goal will initially show a greater awareness of forces related to that change goal than will individuals who are unsuccessful in achieving their change goal.

Expectation of Success. A number of studies in psychotherapy have shown that an individuals' expectations of success or failure can in fact determine his success or failure in therapy (Goldstein 1962, Frank 1963). We would predict that this would be even more likely in a self-directed change project since the individual plays a more central role in his own change effort.

> Hypothesis III. Individuals who are successful in achieving their change goals will show in their initial goal choice papers more indications that they expect success than will individuals who are not successful in achieving their goal.

Psychological Safety. The concept of psychological safety is one which many students of the behavior change process have felt to be essential for successful change (Maslow 1954, Rogers 1951, McClelland 1965, Schein 1968). Rogers gives some insights into how lack of psychological safety (threat) or its presence can effect the goal setting process:

> Any experience which is inconsistent with the organization of the self, (or structure) may be perceived as a threat, and the more of these perceptions there are, the more rigidly the self-structure is organized to maintain itself.
>
> Under certain conditions, involving primarily complete absence of any threat to the self-structure, experiences which are inconsistent with it may be perceived, and examined, and the structure of self revised to assimilate and include such experiences (Rogers 1951, p. 508).

Thus if a person experiences low psychological safety he is likely to defensively distort his weaknesses and be unable to commit himself to new ideals which are different from his present self.

> Hypothesis IV. Individuals who are successful in achieving their change goals will indicate greater psychological safety during the goal-setting process than will individuals who are not successful.

Measurability of the Change Goal. In addition to goal-setting, our previous research on self-directed change has shown that information feedback related to ones change goal is essential for achievement of that goal (Kolb, Winter and Berlew 1968). It seems important, therefore, that a person's change goal be conceived in such a way that feedback from others and the environment could modify it, i.e., it should be measurably. We have already mentioned the Kay, French and Myer study which found improvements in performance only "when specific goals were established with time deadlines set and results measures agreed upon". If an individual has defined his goal in such a way that he can measure whether or not he is achieving it, then he should be more capable of identifying and using feedback.

> Hypothesis V. Individuals who are successful in achieving their change goals will be more likely to progress toward their goal than those who are not successful.

Self-controlled Evaluation. The final hypothesis is related to one of the initial assumptions underlying the self-directed change method -- that changes in behavior are most likely to be successful if the process of changing is seen by the individual to be under his own control. The previously

cited Kay, French and Myer study found that if a subordinate viewed his efforts in the goal setting process as of equal importance and efficacy as his superior's, his achievement of these goals was significantly higher than those who viewed their influence in the process as minimal or less than they deserved. We have already mentioned organizational studies which show the importance of self control in the goal-setting process.

This need for self control of the change process extends beyond initial goal-setting to a need for self control of the process of evaluating progress toward the goal. The studies by Rotter and his associates of internal versus external control of reinforcement (Lefcourt 1966) have found distinct differences between people who see positive and negative events as being a consequence of their own actions and, therefore, under their personal control (Internality) and people who see positive and negative events as caused by external forces and beyond personal control (Externality). Rotter finds that "The individual who has a strong belief that he can control his own destiny is likely to:

a) be more alert to those aspects of the environment which provide useful information for his future behavior

b) takes steps to improve his environmental condition

c) place greater value on skill or achievement reinforcements and be generally more concerned

d) be resistive to subtle attempts to influence him" (Rotter, 1966, p. 25).

Thus from Rotter's research we would predict that individuals who see the evaluation of their progress as being self-controlled and self-reinforced will be more successful than those who see evaluation as being controlled by others.

Rogers, in his attempts to identify the characteristics of effective helping relationships, also stresses the importance of self-evaluation:

I have come to feel that the more I can keep a relationship free of judgment and evaluation, the more this will permit the other person to reach the point where he recognizes that the laws of evaluation, the center of responsibility, lies within himself. The meaning and value of his experience is in the last analysis something which is up to him and no amount of external judgment can alter this" (Rogers, 1961, p. 55).

Hypothesis VIA. Individuals who are successful in achieving their change goals will be more likely to feel that the control of reinforcement that they receive during the change process rests with themselves than those who are not successful.

Hypothesis IVB. Individuals who are successful in achieving their change goals will be less likely to feel that control of reinforcement that they receive during the change process rests with others than those who are not successful.

EXPERIMENTAL PROCEDURE

The experimental procedure used in this study is a modification of earlier applications of the self-directed change method to self-analytic groups (Kolb, Winter and Berlew 1968, Winter, Griffity and Kolb 1968). The setting for the experiment was a semester long course in psychology and human organization, required of Master's candidates in Management at the M.I.T. Sloan School. Offered as an optional part of the course, 111 students participated in 30 hours of T-Group training usually divided into two two-hour sessions each week. There were 8 groups of approximately 15 students each. These groups were structured slightly differently from the traditional T-Group method (see Schein and Bennis, 1965, chapter 3) in that they were focused around a task -- helping one another achieve personal change goals via the self-directed change method. Students chose, at the beginning of the T-Groups individual change goals which they wanted to achieve. They picked goals like having more empathy, being a more effective leader, and taking more; and customarily they shared these goals with other group members asking them for feedback on their progress. This procedure served to define clearly

the groups' task as one of helping others achieve their personal change goals.

The students were about 1/2 undergraduates and 1/2 Master's candidates in Management. There were two females. About 10% of the students were foreign nationals with varying degrees of fluency in the English language. Subjects varied in age from 19 to 35 with most in their early twenties.

Before the T-Groups began students were asked to write a short paper describing how they saw themselves behaving in a group situation and how they would ideally like to behave in the same situation. They were asked to fill out a 60 adjective pair semantic differentials describing their real and ideal selves (see Appendix A). It was made clear to the students that these papers would not affect their course grade.

The students then heard a lecture on self-directed change, including a discussion of factors influencing behavior change and several case studies. After the lecture during the first week of the T-Groups chose change goals relevant to their behavior in groups. Each person was asked to write a short paper describing his goal and answer certain questions regarding the goal and his commitment to it. This goal-choice paper was designed to provide data about the characteristics of the persons initial goal. Students were given the following outline to assist them in writing their papers (the complete form is included in Appendix B).

The Process of Goal Choice:

I. Self-evaluation

1. What are your major strengths and weaknesses in a group as you see them?
2. Are there any areas in which you really want to change?
3. Why do you feel these changes would be desirable?

II. Focusing on one measurable goal

1. Describe as accurately and concretely as possible the goal you have chosen to work toward.
2. What considerations influenced your choice of this particular goal?
3. How do you plan to measure your progress toward this goal? How will you know when you have attained it? What change will be observable to others?

III. Anticipating the Change Process

1. Given your choice of the above goal, what are the factors in yourself, in other people, and in the environment which will help or hinder your progress?

Included with the goal choice paper assignment was a list of the 60 adjective pairs from the real self-ideal self semantic differential. Students were asked to circle those adjective pairs which "best represented the dimensions along which you plan to change". This data was used to determine those aspects of an individual's self-concept which were related to his change goal for testing Hypothesis I.

At the end of each T-Group session each member was asked to fill out a feedback form on which they recorded the feedback they received from others that day. The forms also asked for a daily rating of progress. The purpose of these feedback forms was to stimulate students' awareness of the feedback they were receiving.

The project concluded with a written report by each student on their self-directed change project (see Appendix C). In the report they were asked to describe their change process and their success in achieving their goal. They were also asked to indicate their success in changing on a five point

scale ranging from (1) "I have made no progress in achieving my goal." to (5) "I have completely achieved my goal."

In conjunction with their final report, students completed again the real-self ideal-self semantic differential.

Identification of High Change and Low Change Subjects. Two measures of change were used in this study. The first is based on the discrepancy between real-self descriptions and ideal-self descriptions on the semantic differential. A before discrepancy score was obtained by subtracting the ideal score from the real score of each pair of adjectives on the forms filled out at the beginning of the experiment. An after discrepancy was obtained the same way using the forms filled out at the conclusion of the experiment. To obtain the change score for each adjective pair the magnitude of the after discrepancy was subtracted from the magnitude of the before discrepancy. Thus a positive score would indicate that a person was closer to his ideal-self after his change project than he was before.

An average goal-related change score was then computed for each subject by totalling the change scores for each of the adjective pairs he checked as describing his change goal and dividing by the number of adjective pairs checked. An average non-goal-related change score was computed for each subject by following the same procedure for those adjectives which he did not check. These two scores were used to test hypothesis I.

The second change measure is based on the subjects' self evaluation of their success in achieving their change goal (the five point rating scale included in their final report). This measure was used to test hypothesis about the characteristics of the goal-setting process associated with success or failure in goal achievement. It is used in order to make results gathered here comparable with the results of previous research (Kolb, Winter and Berlew

1968, Winter Griffith and Kolb 1968) which used an experimenter rating of success in goal achievement based on a reading of subjects final reports. The subjects' rating was chosen here because it was felt that the subjects' own rating of his success might more accurately represent his own experience than the experimenter's rating. A comparison of experimenter ratings of the final report with the subjects' ratings show an 85% agreement between the scores. As in previous research a rating of goal achievement on a similar 5 point scale was obtained for each subject from his group leader who received a copy of each individual's change goal at the beginning of the T-Group. The Kendall Tau correlation between these leader ratings and the subject's own ratings was .35 ($p < .01$). Thus, the subject's rating of his success in achieving his goal is consistent with previous research and is related to an observer's rating of his change.

In addition a significant correlation ($r = .39$, $p < .01$) found between the subject's rating of his success and his average goal-related change score on the semantic differential. To form a group of clearly successful and a group of clearly unsuccessful subjects, the 51 individuals who rated themselves as (3) "I have made moderate progress in achieving my goal" were eliminated from further analysis. This left a group of 32 low change subjects who rated themselves (1) "no progress" and (2) "very slight progress", and a group of 28 high change subjects who rated themselves (4) "almost completely achieved my goal" and (5) "completely achieved my goal".

RESULTS

Hypothesis I. Individuals will change more on those dimensions of their self-concept which they define as relevant to their consciously set change goal than they will on dimensions of their self-concept which they define as not relevant. This difference will be independent of the difficulty of the change goal.

The data describing the test of this hypothesis are shown in Table I. Individuals showed an average change of .35 on adjective dimensions related to their goal while showing an average change of .16 on non-goal related dimensions. This difference is highly significant ($p < .005$, 1-tail). An inspection of the adjective pairs that individuals indicated as relevant to their change goal showed that the median number of pairs indicated by an individual was 12 of the 60 adjectives. The number of adjectives indicated ranged from 1 to 46. The median number of times that any single adjective pair was checked was 22 with a range of 4 to 38. From this it can be concluded that individuals tended to use several adjective dimensions to describe their change goal and that all of the 60 adjective dimensions on the semantic differential were used.

To determine whether these differences were simply a result of the fact that subjects tended to choose easy dimensions to change on, a measure of difficulty of change was computed for each adjective dimension. This was accomplished by computing the average change score for each of the 60 adjective dimensions when this dimension was not circled as relevant to the individuals change goal. This change score became an operational definition of difficulty of change without the benefit of goal-setting. The adjectives were rank ordered according to this change score and then divided into three groups of twenty -- a group of easy change adjective dimensions, a moderate group and a group of difficult change dimensions. For each group the mean change per dimension when these adjectives were not goal related was then compared to the mean change when the adjectives were described as goal related. (The reader will note that the sample size is depleted in these comparisons since in some cases, for example, an individual might not describe any easy adjectives as related to his change goal.) The result of these compari-

TABLE I

Self Concept Change in Goal-related and Non-goal-related Dimensions

[1]Wilcoxon matched pairs signed ranc test, 1-tail

sons show significantly more change on goal related dimensions in the easy and difficult dimensions and a similar but small and unsignificant difference in the moderate dimensions. Although the small facilitating effect of goal setting on moderately difficult adjective dimensions is difficult to explain, the facilitating effect shown on both easy and difficult dimensions suggests that the results for all adjective dimensions were not simply a result of choosing easy adjectives.

> Hypothesis II. Individuals who are successful in achieving their change goal will initially show a greater awareness of focus related to that change goal then will individuals who are unsuccessful in achieving their change goal.

The goal choice papers of high change and low change subjects were scored for the number of forces which they mentioned as affecting their change goal. The coding scheme developed by Thomas, Bennis and Fulenwider (1966) was used to score the papers for (1) the total number of focus mentioned, (2) the number of focus which facilitated progress toward the goal, (3) the number of focus which inhibited progress toward the goal, (4) the number of self-related forces, and (5) the number of other-related and environmental focus. The papers were scored on these and all other categories to be described by a scorer who was unaware of the subjects change score. A sample of papers scored by two independend coders showed a 98% agreement in scoring.

The following are examples of the different types of forces scored in the goal-choice papers. The word in parenthesis after the statement describes whether the force was self or other related.

I. Inhibiting Forces:

"I'm not sure about myself and am willing to take anybody's opinion more than I should." (self)

"I'm afraid of letting my feelings be known, I'm afraid of making mistakes in front of the group." (self)

"The main obstacle I face in this goal is the fact that I am (and like to be, i.e., consistant with my ideal) a dominant person." (self)

"If the group is prepared to sit back and just listen obviously I am going to receive little stimulus to improve communication as they do not seem able to reach my level." (others)

"Opposing influences include group attitude toward my self-change project or me." (others)

2. Increasing Forces:

"I have a great desire to become a good effective leader." (self)

"I can accept criticism from others, so that others will accept criticism from me." (self)

"The factors that might help my progress are my innate appreciation for competition and recognition (self), as well as encouragement from the group to initiate ideas." (others)

The average total number of forces and the average number of the various sub-types of forces are shown for High and Low change groups in Table 2. The data confirms the hypothesis that high change subjects show a greater initial awareness of forces relating to their change goal. Although no specific hypotheses were made, the data on the sub-grouping of forces is interesting. The greater awareness of high change subjects seems to be accounted for by their greater awareness of facilitating forces and of other related forces. The greater awareness of facilitating forces suggests that successful goal achievement may be a result of identifying and using those factors which can be of assistance in goal achievement rather than identifying and overcoming obstacles. The greater awareness of other-related forces

TABLE 2

High and Low Change Subject's Awareness
of Forces Related to their Change Goal

	High Change Subjects n = 28	Low Change Subjects n = 32	Significance of difference[1]
Mean Number of forces mentioned	3.69	2.44	< .02
Mean Number of facilitating forces	1.76	.75	< .001
Mean number of inhibiting forces	1.93	1.69	NS
Mean number of self-related forces	2.07	2.03	NS
Mean number of other related forces	1.62	.41	< .0001

[1] Mann Whitney U-Test, 1-tail for total number of forces
2-tail for sub-groupings

suggests that change may be most successful when one sees his deficits as being related not only to himself but to others as well.

> Hypothesis III. Individuals who are successful in achieving their change goals will show in their initial goal choice papers more indications that they expect success than will individuals who are not successful in achieving their goal.

All of the goal choice papers were scored for statements which indicated that the writer expected to be successful in achieving his goal. Statements like the following were scored -- "I expect to achieve my goal by the end of the course." "By the end of the T-Group I expect to achieve my goal." Only explicit statements of expectations of success were scored. Statements of desire for success ("I want to achieve my goal.") or a conditional expectation ("If I can keep active, I expect to arrive at my goal.") were not scored. Two independent scorers showed an 82% agreement on scoring expectations of success. 43% of the subjects in the high change group stated in their goal choice papers that they expected success. Only 9% of the low change subjects stated success expectations. This difference was highly significant ($p < .001$). It is interesting to note that while high change subjects expected more success, they did not see their goal as easier to achieve or that they were closer to it. In response to a question answered at the time of the goal-choice paper that asked how difficult their goal would be to achieve, both high change subjects and low change subjects felt that their goal was moderately difficult (mean ratings of 4.69 and 4.88 respectively on a seven point scale where 7 = "impossible to achieve", Mann-Whitney U-Test significance level = .47). On a seven point scale asking how close they were to their goal (where 7 = goal is achieved) high change and low change subjects had nearly equal mean ratings (3.32 and 3.44 respectively,

Mann Whitney U-Test significance level = .92). Thus success expectations of high change subjects do not appear to be based on their evaluation of the difficulty of their task.

> Hypothesis IV. Individuals who are successful in achieving their change goals will indicate greater psychological safety during the goal-setting process than will individuals who are not successful.

The goal choice papers of high and low change subjects were scored for psychological safety according ot the following scoring category definition:

Negative Statements of Psychological Safety

One point is given for each statement by a person of feeling threatened. This is determined by statements of feelings like shy, withdrawn, ineffective, worthless (feeling unworthy), uneasy in front of people, afraid of others, other's reactions, or himself, and feeling self conscious. General statements of a "lack of self-confidence" were not coded. Evidence of feelings must be present.

Examples of negative statements are:

"I am afraid of not being accepted or included by them."

"This, coupled with my inner feelings of uneasiness in front of a group ...

Positive Statements of Psychological Safety

Minus one point is given for each statement by a person of feeling safe in the environment. This is coded by statements like: feeling successful, having good ideas, and being a good leader.

Examples of positive statements are:

"I find I have the ability to stimulate thought by bringing up cogent questions and comments."

"I feel that my honesty and independence are virtues."

"I see myself as perceptive of group members and motives."

The total psychological safety score equals total negative statements minus total positive statements.

Two independent coders showed a high reliability ($r = .89$, $p < .000$, 2-tailed) on psychological safety scores. Subjects who were successful in achieving their goal had a mean psychological safety score of .28 while unsuccessful subjects had a mean psychological safety score of 1.31 (low scores indicate high psychological safety). The difference between the two groups is significant at the .05 level (1-tail) using the Mann Whitney U-Test. Thus subjects who were successful in changing were more psychologically safe during the initial goal-setting process than subjects who were not successful.

> Hypothesis V. Individuals who are successful in achieving their change goals will be more likely to give consideration to measuring progress toward their goal than those who are not successful.

Although students were instructed to give consideration in their goal choice papers how progress toward their goal might be measured, many did not. The following are examples of subjects who did state a method for measuring their progress:

> I intend to measure my success by two methods: (1) By an intuitive feeling of how much I have contributed to the group activity during a session, and (2) By actually measuring the number of times that I verbally participate during a group meeting.

> My rating system, to be objective, must consist simply of counting the ideas which I propose as a member of the group, with this number being weighted by the relative inventiveness and importance of the idea.

> I plan to measure my progress towards this goal by: 1. Evaluating at the end of each group meeting the level of active close listening, concentration, and clearly thought out and well articulated verbal action that I perceived. 2. Asking others feedback on these three things in particular the latter. Others in the group will perceive me as an active, somewhat influential, articulate, outgoing member as I approach my goal. I am not certain concerning a quantitative manner by which I can keep track of progress. Perhaps if I evaluated each of the three aspects above on a scale from 0 - 100 (as perceived by myself on one graph, and as perceived by others in the group on another graph) this might help me see how I am progressing towards the goal.

The number of high change subjects and low change subjects who mentioned a measurement method were compared. While only 34% of the low change subjects mentioned a method for measuring progress, 79% of the high change subjects mentioned a measurement method. This difference is highly significant ($p < .001$). Giving consideration to how progress toward ones change goal will be measured seems to be a very important part of effective goal-setting.

> Hypothesis VIA. Individuals who are successful in achieving their change goals will be more likely to feel that the control of reinforcement that they receive during the change process rests with themselves than those who are not successful.

> Hypothesis VIB. Individuals who are successful in achieving their change goals will be less likely to feel that control of reinforcement that they receive during the change process rests with others than those who are not successful.

The goal choice papers of high and low change subjects were coded for indications of self evaluation of progress toward their goal and for indications of group evaluation of progress. Examples of self evaluation methods are, "I will record the number of times I speak up in the group on a graph and evaluate my progress after each session", "I will observe how uneasy I feel each time I speak and will know I am progressing toward my goal when I start to feel comfortable", "I will know if I have achieved it (his goal) not through any feedback the group can give me; although the group can confirm it for me, I will know it when I perceive myself acting differently ... only I will know for sure when I've succeeded". Examples of group evaluation methods are, "The group will tell me how at ease I look each time I speak, and whether or not I appear to be improving", "The others in the group will tell me whether or not my statements are coherent and relevant to the subject being discussed".

Two independent scores showed a 90% agreement on both group and self evaluation categories. To test hypothesis VIA the percent of subjects in the

high and low change groups who showed self evaluation methods were compared. 64% of the high change subjects indicated a self evaluation method while only 32% of the low change subjects indicated a self evaluation method ($p < .006$, 1-tail). Hypothesis VIB was tested by comparing the percent of subjects in the high and low change groups who indicated group evaluation methods. 28% of the low change subjects indicated a group evaluation method while 32% of the high change subjects indicated a group evaluation method. This difference was not in the direction predicted and was not statistically significant. Thus it appears that self-controlled evaluation facilitates goal achievement while group controlled evaluation is unrelated to goal achievement.

CONCLUSIONS AND IMPLICATIONS

The experiment presents convincing evidence that conscious goal-setting plays an important role in the process of self-directed behavior change. Individuals tend to change more in those areas of their self-concept which are related to their consciously set change goals. These changes are independent of the difficulty of the change goal and thus do not appear to be a result of an initial choice of easy to achieve goals. The results would suggest a modification of those Freudian and learning theory based approaches to behavior change that treat consciousness as an epiphenomen by placing heavy emphasis on unconscious forces and behavioral conditioning. While this experiment, since it does not involve an experimental manipulation of goal setting, does not conclusively prove that conscious goal-setting caused the subsequent changes in self-concept, taken with other experimental studies cited in this paper it does strongly suggest that conscious goal-setting facilitates goal achievement.

The analysis of the initial goal descriptions of subjects who were subsequently successful and unsuccessful in achieving their goals provides evidence for those specific characteristics of the goal setting process which are crucial for goal achievement. Awareness of forces related to the change goal, high expectations of success, high psychological safety, a concern for measuring progress, and an emphasis on self-controlled evaluation all appear to be precursors of successful goal achievement.

While the data in this experiment are not sufficiently quantified to allow tests of the interrelationships among the variables identified as important characteristics of the goal-setting process, the results suggest some tentative outlines for a cybernetic model of behavior change. Nearly

every student of personality and behavior change has recognized that human personality is a dynamic feedback system with self-sustaining and self-reinforcing qualities. Sullivan, for example, sees this aspect of personality (which he calls the self system) to be the major stumbling block to constructive personality change. Hall and Lindsey (1957) describe his concept of the self system this way:

> The self system as the guardian of one's security tends to become isolated from the rest of the personality; it excludes information that is incongruous with its present organization and fails thereby to profit from experience. Since the self guards the person from anxiety, it is held in high esteem and protected from criticism. As the self system grows in complexity and independence it prevents the person from making objective judgements of his own behavior and it glosses over obvious contradictions between what the person really is and what his self system says he is" (p. 139).

Since individuals tend to act in accord with their self-system, threats to the self system will cause a person's activities to become more and more inappropriate and rigid leading to further failure and insecurity which in turn leads to further distortions in the self system and so on. A key variable in this process is security or what we have called psychological safety. The characteristics of the goal-setting process which have found to be associated with successful self directed change give some clues about the nature of this relationship between psychological safety and change. Figure 1 shows how the goal setting characteristics might fit into a cybernetic model of the change process. Interrelationships among the variables are simplified to illustrate the dominant feedback loop. For purpose of illustration, these characteristics describe an unsuccessful change process beginning with low psychological safety. Low psychological safety can lead to decreased awareness which this research suggests may take the form of a preoccupation with oneself at the expense of environmental and other forces

FIGURE I

A Simple Cybernetic Model of
Behavior Change and Helping Interventions

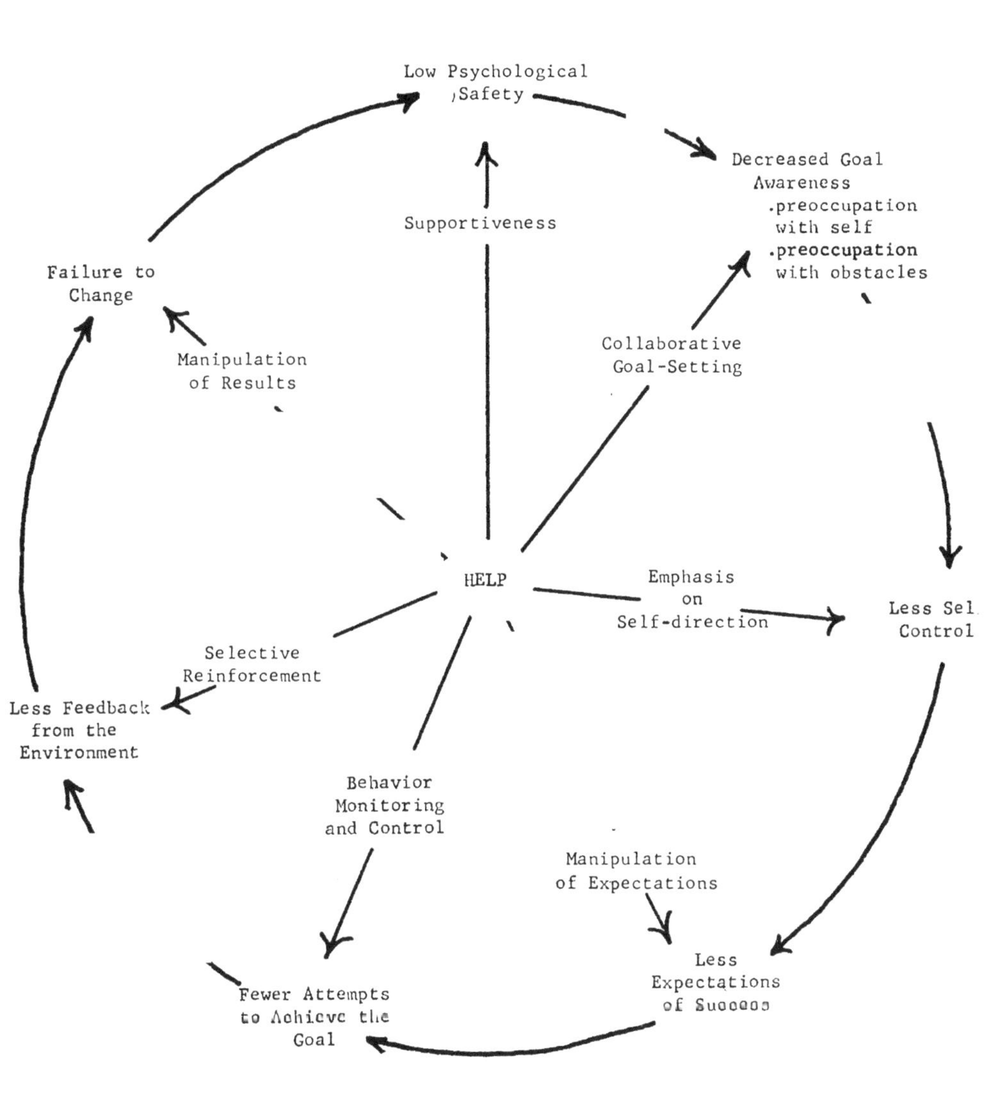

and a preoccupation with obstacles to change at the expense of forces which would facilitate change. This decrease in awareness would in turn lead to a decreased sense of self-control which would lead to fewer expectations of success. Low expectations of success would produce few attempts to achieve the goal which would in turn produce fewer opportunities for feedback from the environment. All this would tend to produce failure in achieving the goal. The failure feelings thus aroused would tend to further decrease psychological safety producing an amplification of this positive feedback loop.

Implications for Helping Interventions.

This cybernetic model of the behavior change process suggests several intervention strategies that may serve to create more effective helping relationships. Since feedback loops are composed of elements which need not have a prior or an hierarchical causal order, helping interventions can be directed to the point or points in the feedback loop where they will be most effective in producing change. As Phillips and Wiener put it:

> Within the cybernetic framework, although not unique to it, variables are selected and regulated in the feedback chain which are most amenable to manipulation and control. In structured therapy, elusive causes are not sought that might operate to produce a disordered system: the therapist goes directly to the element (information) in the feedback loop that has a meaningful coefficient of efficiency in maintaining the loop, and he proceeds immediately to try to insert the change (1966, p. 96).

Thus, cybernetic models of the change process hold forth the promise of an eclectic approach to the choice of helping strategies based on research which identifies those elements in the feedback loop which have the highest "coefficient of efficiency".

The simplified model of change shown in Figure 1 suggests seven types of intervention which may prove effective in breaking into the self defeating cycle of failure

1. Supportiveness. Rogerian theory has been based primarily on the supportive strategy of increasing the clients' security and self confidence through the therapists' unconditional positive regard, accurate empathy, and genuineness (Rogers 1961). Truax and his associates (Truax and Carkhuff 1964) have shown that these three therapist characteristics are related to constructive personality change in both Rogerian and other forms of therapy. In addition they find that the presence of these variables in the therapist are positively related to interpersonal exploration on the part of the patient. These results suggest that supportive interventions aimed at increasing psychological safety have a relatively higher coefficient of efficiency in that they produce positive change and gains in another element in the feedback loop -- awareness (intrapersonal exploration).

2. Collaborative goal-setting. Attempts to increase awareness of personal improvement goals through an explicit process of collaborative goal-setting have not often been a part of behavior change programs. However, the use of this strategy in achievement motivation training programs and in organizational settings as well as in research on self-directed behavior change suggests that goal-setting procedures may indeed be a highly effective intervention method. In fact, a careful examination of behavior therapy method of change suggests that in addition to applying for example the principles of recipricol inhibition (Wolpe 1958) the therapist is also leading the patient through a process of explicit goal-setting. By asking the patient to define and rank order the fear evoking situations in his life and then telling him to try to relax while visualizing the weakest fear situation until he masters it and then proceeding to the next weakest and so on; the therapist is in effect helping the patient to set realistic goals and work to achieve them in a way that is quite similar to the self-directed change

method. At this point no research evidence exists which can tell us whether it is the process of recipricol inhibition or collaborative goal-setting which is the change producing intervention. Similar questions can be raised about other behavior therapy methods.

3. Emphasis on Self-direction. While few therapeutic systems place a heavy emphasis on self control of the change process in their methodology (with the possible exception of Kelly, 1955) it is a common assumption that true psychotherapeutic change does not occur until the patient works through his dependence upon the therapist and achieves self-direction. The literature on cognitive dissonance gives experimental evidence for the importance of self-direction in attitude change. These experiments show that attitude change is greatest and most enduring when the person feels that he has freely chosen to alter his point of view (Secord and Backman 1964). Recognizing the importance of self-direction in personality change, self-help societies like Alcoholics Anonymous and Synanon (for narcotics addicts) have made the principles of personal responsibility and voluntary commitment to change a central part of their ideology.

4. Manipulation of expectations. Research evidence on the impact of an individual's expectations on his own chances for successful change has already been presented. As yet few direct attempts have been made to directly increase individual's expectations of success. A significant exception is the previously cited work on achievement motivation training. That manipulation of expectations can produce change is shown by a well-executed study by Rosenthal and Jacobson (1968). They found that intellectual gains could be produced in children by nothing more than giving names of children who had been selected at random to their new teachers at the beginning of the school year and describing them to the teachers as children who could be expected

to show unusual gains in intellignece during the year. This research suggests that helping interventions that increase expectations of success may be a very effective metnod of breaking the cycle of failure.

5. Behavior monitoring and control. Behavior therapy attempts to elicit behaviors consistent with constructive personality change goals are of two types -- stimulus control and modeling (Schwitzgebel and Kolb, in press). In stimulus control methods environmental conditions which serve as either discriminating or eliciting stimuli for desired behavioral responses are used to increase the probability of a desired response, or decrease a response to be avoided. A simple example would be the case of the student who moves his study area away from his bed in order to keep from falling asleep. Modeling can be defined as "the systematic procision of opportunities for observing the behavior of others, wherein the cues to behavior came from the behavior of others. In short, this is "vicarious learning" (Brayfield, 1968, p. 480). A number of studies, most notably by Bandura and Walters (1963), have shown that the observation of a given behavior in a model increases the occurance of that behavior.

In self-directed behavior change projects another method has been successfully used to elicit goal directed behavior -- behavior monitoring. By keeping continuous record of progress toward their goal subjects are constantly reminded of the goal they are trying to achieve thus producing more attempts to achieve that goal (Zachs 1965, Goldiamond 1965, Schwitzgebel 1964). The fact that high change subjects in the research presented in this paper gave more attention than low change subjects to how their progress could be measured provides additional evidence for the efficiency of behavior monitoring procedures.

6. Selective reinforcement. Perhaps the best documented strategy for producing change is the manipulation of environmental feedback through the use of selective reinforcement. The methods of operant shaping and intermittent positive reinforcement have been used to alter such insignificant behaviors as use of pronouns and such major behavioral patterns as delinquent behavior and schizophrenic symptoms (Schwitzgebel and Kolb, in press). Research on self-directed change suggests that in certain circumstances the total amount of information feedback may also be related to change (Kolb, Winter and Berlew, 1968).

7. Manipulation of results. A final intervention method which deserves consideration is the manipulation of results of change. While this method has not been used systematically as a therapeutic intervention, it is a common device in experimental research. For example, the literature on level of aspiration is replete with examples of artificial manipulation of performance results, which show measurable changes in future goal-setting and performance. While there are obvious problems of credibility for the change agent with such artificial distortions of reality this method may prove to be a promising helping strategy.

It can be seen from the above discussion that the elements of the goal-setting process that are crucial for successful goal achievement as well as feedback from the environment and the final change score itself may all be changed by helping interventions. The task for future research is to determine how effective these interventions, taken singly or in combination can be in changing the cycle of insecurity and failure to one of psychological safety and success. The most effective intervention strategy may well prove to be behavior therapy approaches in combination with the goal-setting procedures of self-directed change.

APPENDIX A

Name________________________________

On this page you will find a set of adjective dimensions which people have used to describe themselves. Place a checkmark (√) in the appropriate space along each dimension to best describe yourself <u>as you really are</u> in a group. If a dimension does not apply, place a checkmark in the middle space. There are no right or wrong answers. This form is another means of helping you to look at yourself.

Accepted	:___:___:___:___:___:___:___:	Rejected
Active	:___:___:___:___:___:___:___:	Passive
Accept Criticism	:___:___:___:___:___:___:___:	Reject Criticism
Affectionate	:___:___:___:___:___:___:___:	Unaffectionate
Anxious	:___:___:___:___:___:___:___:	Relaxed
Attentive	:___:___:___:___:___:___:___:	Inattentive
Autocratic	:___:___:___:___:___:___:___:	Democratic
Awkward	:___:___:___:___:___:___:___:	Poised
Cautious	:___:___:___:___:___:___:___:	Daring
Central	:___:___:___:___:___:___:___:	Peripheral
Close	:___:___:___:___:___:___:___:	Distant
Confident	:___:___:___:___:___:___:___:	Not Confident
Cynical	:___:___:___:___:___:___:___:	Not Cynical
Dependent	:___:___:___:___:___:___:___:	Independent
Disloyal	:___:___:___:___:___:___:___:	Loyal
Disorganized	:___:___:___:___:___:___:___:	Organized
Disruptive	:___:___:___:___:___:___:___:	Harmonious
Dominant	:___:___:___:___:___:___:___:	Submissive
Effective	:___:___:___:___:___:___:___:	Ineffective
Emotional	:___:___:___:___:___:___:___:	Unemotional
Excluded	:___:___:___:___:___:___:___:	Included
Flexible	:___:___:___:___:___:___:___:	Rigid
Follower	:___:___:___:___:___:___:___:	Leader
Frank	:___:___:___:___:___:___:___:	Guarded
Good listener	:___:___:___:___:___:___:___:	Poor listener
Humerous	:___:___:___:___:___:___:___:	Humorless
Impatient	:___:___:___:___:___:___:___:	Patient
Inarticulate	:___:___:___:___:___:___:___:	Articulate
Influential	:___:___:___:___:___:___:___:	Not influential
Inhibited	:___:___:___:___:___:___:___:	Uninhibited

(continued)

Name________________________________

Important	:___:___:___:___:___:___:___:	Unimportant
Insincere	:___:___:___:___:___:___:___:	Sincere
Liked	:___:___:___:___:___:___:___:	Disliked
Like people	:___:___:___:___:___:___:___:	Dislike people
Make friends easily	:___:___:___:___:___:___:___:	Do not make friends easily
Outgoing	:___:___:___:___:___:___:___:	Retiring
Perceptive	:___:___:___:___:___:___:___:	Imperceptive
Personal	:___:___:___:___:___:___:___:	Impersonal
Pessimistic	:___:___:___:___:___:___:___:	Optimistic
Prefer to listen	:___:___:___:___:___:___:___:	Prefer to talk
Reject others' ideas	:___:___:___:___:___:___:___:	Accept others' ideas
Satisfied	:___:___:___:___:___:___:___:	Dissatisfied
Secretive	:___:___:___:___:___:___:___:	Open
Self conscious	:___:___:___:___:___:___:___:	Not self conscious
Sensitive	:___:___:___:___:___:___:___:	Insensitive
Spontaneous	:___:___:___:___:___:___:___:	Inhibited
Successful	:___:___:___:___:___:___:___:	Unsucessful
Superior	:___:___:___:___:___:___:___:	Inferior
Sympathetic	:___:___:___:___:___:___:___:	Unsympathetic
Tactless	:___:___:___:___:___:___:___:	Tactful
Talkative	:___:___:___:___:___:___:___:	Quiet
Timid	:___:___:___:___:___:___:___:	Aggressive
Tolerant	:___:___:___:___:___:___:___:	Intolerant
Trusting	:___:___:___:___:___:___:___:	Suspicious
Trustworthy	:___:___:___:___:___:___:___:	Untrustworthy
Unfriendly	:___:___:___:___:___:___:___:	Friendly
Unoriginal	:___:___:___:___:___:___:___:	Original
Warm	:___:___:___:___:___:___:___:	Cool
Weak	:___:___:___:___:___:___:___:	Strong
Withdrawn	:___:___:___:___:___:___:___:	Involved

Name________________________________

On this page you will find an identical set of adjective dimensions. Place a checkmark (√) in the space along each dimension to best describe the ideal version of yourself, i.e. you as you would like to be in a group. If a dimension does not apply, place a checkmark in the middle space. There should be a checkmark on each line. Again there are no right or wrong answers.

Accepted :___:___:___:___:___:___:___: Rejected
Active :___:___:___:___:___:___:___: Passive
Accept Criticism :___:___:___:___:___:___:___: Reject Criticism
Affectionate :___:___:___:___:___:___:___: Unaffectionate
Anxious :___:___:___:___:___:___:___: Relaxed

Attentive :___:___:___:___:___:___:___: Inattentive
Autocratic :___:___:___:___:___:___:___: Democratic
Awkward :___:___:___:___:___:___:___: Poised
Cautious :___:___:___:___:___:___:___: Daring
Central :___:___:___:___:___:___:___: Peripheral

Close :___:___:___:___:___:___:___: Distant
Confident :___:___:___:___:___:___:___: Not Confident
Cynical :___:___:___:___:___:___:___: Not Cynical
Dependent :___:___:___:___:___:___:___: Independent
Disloyal :___:___:___:___:___:___:___: Loyal

Disorganized :___:___:___:___:___:___:___: Organized
Disruptive :___:___:___:___:___:___:___: Harmonious
Dominant :___:___:___:___:___:___:___: Submissive
Effective :___:___:___:___:___:___:___: Ineffective
Emotional :___:___:___:___:___:___:___: Unemotional

Excluded :___:___:___:___:___:___:___: Included
Flexible :___:___:___:___:___:___:___: Rigid
Follower :___:___:___:___:___:___:___: Leader
Frank :___:___:___:___:___:___:___: Guarded
Good listener :___:___:___:___:___:___:___: Poor listener

Humerous :___:___:___:___:___:___:___: Humorless
Impatient :___:___:___:___:___:___:___: Patient
Inarticulate :___:___:___:___:___:___:___: Articulate
Influential :___:___:___:___:___:___:___: Not influential
Inhibited :___:___:___:___:___:___:___: Uninhibited

(continued)

Name________________________________

Important :___:___:___:___:___:___:___: Unimportant
Insincere :___:___:___:___:___:___:___: Sincere
Liked :___:___:___:___:___:___:___: Disliked
Like people :___:___:___:___:___:___:___: Dislike people
Make friends easily :___:___:___:___:___:___:___: Do not make friends easily

Outgoing :___:___:___:___:___:___:___: Retiring
Perceptive :___:___:___:___:___:___:___: Imperceptive
Personal :___:___:___:___:___:___:___: Impersonal
Pessimistic :___:___:___:___:___:___:___: Optimistic
Prefer to listen :___:___:___:___:___:___:___: Prefer to talk

Reject others' ideas :___:___:___:___:___:___:___: Accept others' ideas
Satisfied :___:___:___:___:___:___:___: Dissatisfied
Secretive :___:___:___:___:___:___:___: Open
Self conscious :___:___:___:___:___:___:___: Not self conscious
Sensitive :___:___:___:___:___:___:___: Insensitive

Spontaneous :___:___:___:___:___:___:___: Inhibited
Successful :___:___:___:___:___:___:___: Unsuccessful
Superior :___:___:___:___:___:___:___: Inferior
Sympathetic :___:___:___:___:___:___:___: Unsympathetic
Tactless :___:___:___:___:___:___:___: Tactful

Talkative :___:___:___:___:___:___:___: Quiet
Timid :___:___:___:___:___:___:___: Aggressive
Tolerant :___:___:___:___:___:___:___: Intolerant
Trusting :___:___:___:___:___:___:___: Suspicious
Trustworthy :___:___:___:___:___:___:___: Untrustworthy

Unfriendly :___:___:___:___:___:___:___: Friendly
Unoriginal :___:___:___:___:___:___:___: Original
Warm :___:___:___:___:___:___:___: Cool
Weak :___:___:___:___:___:___:___: Strong
Withdrawn :___:___:___:___:___:___:___: Involved

APPENDIX B

The lecture on self-directed change and the real-self -- ideal-self papers have been intended to stimulate your thinking in areas of self-development and personal change. We would like you to select a change goal toward which you can work during the forthcoming T-Group sessions. This "self-research" project should be in some area of personal or interpersonal behavior which can be explored in a group; those whose projects are carried out within the T-Group benefit from feedback from other group members.

If you do not have an appropriate goal or change project in mind, it may be helpful for you to study the three phases of the process of goal choice as outlined below. The outline and questions are not intended to be restrictive; we present them only to raise some issues which others have found important in their choices of a change project and goal:

The Process of Goal Choice

I. Self-evaluation

1. What are your major strengths and weaknesses in a group as you see them?
2. Are there any areas in which you really want to change?
3. Why do you feel these changes would be desirable?

II. Focusing on one measurable goal

1. Describe as accurately and concretely as possible the goal you have chosen to work toward.
2. What considerations influenced your choice of this particular goal?
3. How do you plan to measure your progress toward this goal? How will you know when you have attained it? What change will be observable to others?

III. Anticipating the change proces

Given your choice of the above goals, what are the factors in yourself, in other people, and in the environment which will help or hinder your progress?

When you have chosen a change goal, write a short paper describing this goal in detail. Try to define a change dimension that is reasonably narrow and specific rather than very broad or general. Define also any other aspects of your project that you think may be relevant (e.g., observation and measurement of variables, measurement of progress, forces working for and against change). The outline above may be helpful here.

After your paper is completed, fill out the following three pages of this handout and hand them in with your paper.

The change project papers, the 2 question sheets, and the adjective pair list are due November 15. They are required from all students participating in T-Groups, but will not be used in determining course grades.

To further clarify the nature of change projects and goals, we have listed below several examples of self-change projects; again, this list is for the purpose of illustration; it is not restrictive and the examples are not collectively exhaustive.

Some examples of change goals:

"I would like to be more assertive and forceful, and to act this way comfortably. I would like to fight more effectively with others."
"I would like to be less assertive and agressive, and to be comfortable while acting this way."
"My concerns about hurting other people's feelins often inhibit me from doing and saying what I think ought to be said and done. I would like to be sensitive to others' feelings without letting this sensitivity inhibit me."
"I would like to express warmth and affection more comfortably. I would like to communicate to others that I like them."
"I would like to risk losing friendships in order to do what is right -- to be less concerned about hurting those I like."

"I would like to be more comfortable with unclarity and confusion -- to tolerate silence, lack of structure, lack of clear-cut plan or order."

"I would like to be more rational, more ordered -- to put mine and others' experiences in some logical, ordered framework of understanding."

"I would like to challenge and deal with authority figures more effectively and comfortably."

"I would like to deal with subordinates in a more satisfactory manner."

"I would like to express myself more openly, frankly and spontaneously -- to do less censoring of my ideas and feelings."

Name ______________________

My goal is ____

____

Below are several questions which pertain to your personal feelings about the change project you have just chosen. Check each scale in the appropriate space.

1. How committed are you to changing toward the goal you have choses?

committed								very much uncommitted

2. How confident are you in your ability to change?

very confident								not at all confidnet

3. How close are you to your goal right now?

as far from my goal as possible								have achieved my goal

4. How "safe" do you feel in exposing your change project to your T-Group?

not very safe								very safe

5. Have you previously or informally tried to change your attitudes or behavior along the lines of your present change project? Yes ___ No ___

6. Some people select a change project which they consider "easy" to achieve while others pick change goals chich they feel will be "impossible" to attain. How difficult do you feel your change goal will be?

easy to achieve								impossible to achieve
			moderate		challenging			

7. Your T-Group will probably feel that your change goal is:

easy to achieve								impossible to achieve
			moderate		challenging			

8. How will your T-Group probably feel about your choice of a change project? Circle one.

   a. They will probably be strongly favorable to my choice.
   b. They will probably be slightly favorable to my choice.
   c. They will probably be indifferent to my choice.
   d. They will probably be slightly opposed to my choice.
   e. They will probably be strongly opposed to my choice.

9. The behavior specified by my change goal is:

   a. Close to my present behavior.
   b. Somewhere between my present behavior and my ideal for behavior.
   c. Close to my ideal for behavior.
   d. Precisely my ideal for behavior.

Name

Below is a list of adjective pairs which describe certain aspects of personality, interpersonal relationships, and T-Group experiences. Circle the <u>pairs</u> of adjectives which best represent the dimensions along which you plan to change. It is possible that several adjective pairs (or perhaps none at all) are related to your project, so examine the whole list carefully.

accept others' ideas: reject others ideas

aggressive: timid

articulate: inarticulate

cool: warm

daring: cautious

democratic: autocratic

dislike people: like people

disliked: liked

dissatisfied: satisfied

distant: close

do not make friends easily: make friends easily

friendly: unfriendly

guarded: frank

harmonious: disruptive

humorless: humorous

imperceptive: perceptive

impersonal: personal

inattentive: attentive

included: excluded

independent: dependent

ineffective: effective

inferior: superior

inhibited: spontaneous

insensitive: sensitive

intolerant: tolerant

involved: withdrawn

leader: follower

loyal: disloyal

not confident: confident

not cynical: cynical

not influential: influential

not self-conscious: self-conscious

open: secretive

optomistic: pessimistic

organized: disorganized

original: unoriginal

passive: active

patient: impatient

peripheral: central

poised: awkward

poor listener: good listener

prefer to talk: prefer to listen

quiet: talkative

reject criticism: accept criticism

rejected: accepted

relaxed: anxious

retiring: outgoing

rigid: flexible

sincere: insincere

strong: weak

submissive: dominent

suspicious: trusting

tactful: tactless

unaffectionate: affectionate

unemotional: emotional

unimportant: important

uninhibited: inhibited

unsuccessful: successful

unsympathetic: sympathetic

untrustworthy: trustworthy

CHANGE PROJECT REPORTS

A short paper describing the results of your self-change project will be due on Tuesday, December 20. This paper is required from all students participating in T-Groups. Although this report need not be long, it should be carefully prepared. It may be structured in any way you choose, but each of the following questions should be fully discussed:

1. Without looking at your original description of your change goal attempt to describe your change goal as you currently see it. Compare this description with your original project choice. Do you see your change project differently now than you did at the start? How do you account for these differences, if there are any?

2. Do you feel you have changed this semester? If so, how?

3. What factors facilitated or hindered progress on your change project?

4. Do you feel that any specific type (or types) of feedback helped you change? Did any type cause you to modify your goal?

It is not necessary to have changed in order to write a good change report. Most important is an understanding of why a change did or did not take place, and how this process occurred.

After completing your paper, fill in the following pages which are referred to as Appendix I, II, III, and IV _and attach them to your paper_. Papers and appendices should be handed in together to your trainer if your group is meeting on Tuesday; if your group is not meeting on Tuesday then papers should be submitted to Professor Kolb's secretary in Room E52-560. All reports are due by 4:00 pm, December 20.

Name ______________________________ Group ____________

APPENDIX I

1. In previous project reports, some students maintained the same change goal throughout the semester while other students modified their original goal in various ways. Circle the one statement that most appropriately represents your project.

   a. My goal remained the same as initially stated.
   b. My goal remained basically the same, but I've lowered my aspirations.
   c. My goal remained basically the same, but I've raised my aspirations.
   d. I expanded my goal to include other areas in addition to the one originally chosen.
   e. My original goal was too broad, I restricted it to contain one or two elements of my original goal.
   f. I abandoned my original goal and selected a new one.
   g. I abandoned my goal entirely and did not select a new one.

2. If your goal was modified, indicate on the time scale below the approximate period that it changed.

|________|________|________|________|________|________|________|

Statement of Original goal — Last sess of T-Gro

3. Have you achieved your goal as originally stated? Circle one.

   a. I have made no progress in achieving my goal.
   b. I have made very slight progress in achieving my goal.
   c. I have made moderate progress in achieving my goal.
   d. I have almost completely achieved my goal.
   e. I have completely achieved my goal.

4. How do you think your T-Croup felt about your change goal?

|________|________|________|________|________|________|________|

Easy to Achieve — Moderate — Challenging — Impossib to Achie

5. Was your T-Group:

   a. Strongly favorable to your choice of a change goal.
   b. Slightly favorable to your choice of a change goal.
   c. Indifferent to your choice.
   d. Slightly opposed to your choice.
   e. Strongly opposed to your choice.

6. How involved were you in your change project? Circle one.

Very Uninvolved 1_____2_____3_____4_____5_____6_____7_____8_____9 Very Involved

7. On the average, how confident were you that you could achieve your change goal. Circle one

Very Unconfident 1_____2_____3_____4_____5_____6_____7_____8_____9 Very Confident

8. On the average, how committed were you to reaching your goal? Circle one.

Very Uncommitted 1_____2_____3_____4_____5_____6_____7_____8_____9 Very Committed

9. How "safe" did you feel in exposing your change project to your T-Group?

|______|______|______|______|______|______|______|______|

Not Very Safe   Very Safe

APPENDIX II

Below is a list of adjective pairs which describe certain aspects of personality, interpersonal relationships, and T-Group experiences. Circle the pairs of adjectives which you not feel were most related to your original change project. It is possible that several adjective pairs (or perhaps none at all) are related to your project, so examine the whole list carefully.

accepted: rejected
active: passive
accept criticism: reject criticism
affectionate: unaffectionate
anxious: relaxed
attentive: inattentive
autocratic: democratic
awkward: poised
cautious: daring
central: peripheral
close: distant
confident: not confident
cynical: not cyncial
dependent: independent
disloyal: loyal
disorganized: organized
disruptive: harmonious
dominant: submissive
effective: ineffective
emotional: unemotional
excluded: included
flexible: rigid
follower: leader
frank: guarded
good listener; poor listener
humorous: humorless
impatient: patient
inarticulate: articulate
influential: not influential
inhibited: uninhibited

important: unimportant
insincere: sincere
liked: disliked
like people: dislike people
make friends easily: do not make friends easily
outgoing: retiring
perceptive: imperceptive
personal: impersonal
pessimistic: optimistic
prefer to listen: prefer to talk
reject others' ideas: accept others ideas
satisfied: dissatisfied
secretive: open
self-conscious: not self-conscious
sensitive: insensitive
spontaneous: inhibited
successful: unsuccessful
superior: inferior
sympathetic: unsympathetic
tactless: tactful
talkative: quiet
timid: aggressive
tolerant: intolerant
trusting: suspicious
trustworthy: untrustworthy
unfriendly: friendly
unoriginal: original
warm: cool
weak: strong
withdrawn: involved

BIBLIOGRAPHY

Allport, G.W. Personality and Social Encounter. Boston: Beacon Press, 1960.

Atkinson, J.W. (Ed.). Motives in Fantasy, Action and Society. New Jersey: Van Nostrand, 1958.

Bandura, A. and R.H. Walters. Social Learning and Personality Development. New York: Holt, Rinehart and Winston, 1963.

Bennis, Thomas, Fulenwider. "Problem Analysis Diagram", Sloan School of Management, M.I.T.

Brayfield, A. "Human Resources Development", American Psychologist, Vol. 23, No. 7, pp. 479-482, 1968.

Drucker, P.F. The Practice of Management. New York: Harper Brothers, 1954.

Festinger, L. "A Theoretical Interpretation of Shifts in Level of Aspiration", Psychological Review, Vol. 49, pp. 235-250, 1942.

Frank, J.D. "Recent Studies of the Level of Aspiration", Psychological Bulletin, Vol. 38, pp. 218-226, 1941.

Frank, J.D. Persuasion and Healing. New York: Schoeken Books, 1963.

Gendlin, Eugene, J. Beebe III, J. Cassens, M. Klein and M. Gaerlander. "Focusing ability in psychotherapy, personality and creativity", Shlein, J. (Ed.), Research in Psychotherapy, Vol. III, American Psychological Assocination, Washington, D.C., 1968.

Goldiamond, I. "Self-control Procedures in Personal Behavior Problems", Psychological Reports, Vol. 17, pp. 851-868, 1965.

Goldstein, A. Therapist-patient Expectancies in Psychotherapy. New York: Pergamon Press, 1962.

Hartman, H. E. Kris and R.M. Loewenstein. "Comments on the Formation of Psychic Structure", Anna Freud et.al. (Eds.), The *Psychoanalytic Study of the Child*. New York: International University Press, Vol. 2, 1947.

Hall, C.S., G. Lindzey. *Theories of Personality*. New York: John Wiley and Sons, Inc., 1957.

James, William. *Psychology*. Greenwich, Connecticut: Fawcett Publications, 1963.

Kausler, D.H. "Aspiration Level as a Determinant of Performance", *J. of Personality*, Vol. 27, pp. 346-351, 1959.

Kay, French and Meyer. *A Study of the Performance Appraisal Interview*, Management Development and Employee Relations Services, General Electric, New York, 1962.

Kelley, G.A. *The Psychology of Personal Constructs*. New York: Norton Press, 1955.

Kolb, D.A. "Achievement Motivation Training for Under-Achieving High School Boys", *J. of Personality and Social Psychology*, Vol. 2, No. 6, pp. 783-792, 1965.

Kolb, D.A., S. Winter and J.C. Griffith. "Capacity for Self-direction", *J. of Consulting and Clinical Psychology*, Vol. 32, No. 1, pp. 35-41, 1968.

Kolb, D.A., S. Winter and D. Berlew. "Self-directed Change: Two Studies", *J. of Applied Behavioral Sciences*, (in press), 1968.

Kolb, D.A., and Ralph Schwitzgebel. *Changing Human Behavior*. New York: Van Nostrand, (in press).

Lefcourt, H.M. "Internal Versus External Control of Reinforcement", *Psych. Bulletin*, Vol. 65, No. 4, pp. 206-220, 1966.

Lewin, Dembo, Festinger, Sears. "Legal of Aspiration", J. McV. Hunt (Ed.), *Personality and Behavior Disorders*. New York: Ronald, pp. 333-378, 1944.

Likert, R. The Human Organization. New York: McGraw-Hill, Company, 1967.

Litwin, G., J. Aronoff. "Achievement Motivation Training and Executive Advancement", J. of Applied Behavioral Science, (in press), 1968.

Lorenz, K. On Aggression. New York: Harcourt, Brace and World, Inc. 1963.

Maslow, A. Motivation and Personality. New York: Harper Brothers, 1954.

Milgram, S. "Behavioral Study of Obedience", Bennis et.al. (Eds.), Interpersonal Dynamics. Homewood, Illinois: Dorsey Press, 1968.

McClelland, D.C. The Achieving Society. New York: Van Nostrand, 1961.

McClelland, D.C. "Toward a Theory of Motive Acquisition", American Psychologist, Vol. 20, pp. 321-333, 1965.

McGregor, D. The Human Side of Enterprise. New York: McGraw-Hill Co., 1960.

Orne, M. "On the Social Psychology of the Psychological Experiment: With Particular Reference to Demand Characteristics and Their Implications", American Psychologist, Vol. 17, pp. 776-783, 1962.

Phillips, E.L. and D. Wiener. Short-term Psychotherapy and Structured Behavior Change. New York: McGraw-Hill Co., 1966.

Rao, K.U. "The Effect of Interference with Certain Aspects of Goal-setting on Level of Aspiration Behavior", Psychological Studies, Vol. 1, pp. 1-10, 1959.

Rogers, C.R. Client'centered Therapy. Boston: Houghton-Mifflin Co., 1951.

Rogers, C.R. On Becoming a Person. Boston: Houghton-Mifflin Co., 1961.

Rosenthal,R. "On the Social Psychology of the Psychological Experiment: The Experimenter's Hypothesis as Unintended Determinant of Experimental Results", American Scientist, Vol. 51, pp. 268-283, 1963.

Rosenthal, R. and Jacobson. "Teacher Expectations for the Disadvantaged", Scientific American, Vol. 218, No. 4, pp. 19-23, 1968.

Rotter, J.B. "Generalized Expectancies for Internal Versus External Control of Reinforcement", Psychological Monographs, Vol. 80, No.1, 1966.

Schein, E.H. "Personal Change Through Interpersonal Relationships", Bennis et.al. (Eds.), Interpersonal Dynamics. Homewood, Illinois, 1968.

Schwitzgebel, R. "A Simple Behavioral System for Recording and Implementing Change in Natural Settings", unpublished doctoral dissertation, Harvard School of Education, 1964.

Truax, C., R. Carkhoff. "For Better or For Worse: The Process of Psychotherapeutic Personality Change", Recent Advances in the Study of Behavior Change. Montreal: McGill University Press, pp. 118-163, 1964.

White, R.W. "Motivation Reconsidered: The Concept of Competence", Psychological Review, Vol. 66, pp. 297-333, 1959.

Wolpe, J. Psychotherapy by Reciprocal Inhibition. Stanford: Stanford University Press, 1958.

Zachs, J. "Collaborative Therapy for Smokers", unpublished manuscript, Harvard University, 1965.

ND - #0040 - 210323 - C0 - 229/152/6 [8] - CB - 9780484330305 - Gloss Lamination